THE BEGINNERS GUIDEBOOK TO MENTAL TOUGHNESS TRAINING FOR MARATHON RUNNERS:

PEAK PERFORMANCE THROUGH MEDITATION, CALMNESS OF MIND, AND STRESS MANAGEMENT

By

Joseph Correa

Certified Meditation Instructor

Copyright

Acknowledgements

This book is dedicated to all the people that made a difference in my life and the knowledge they shared throughout the years. Thank you.

Contents

THE BEGINNERS GUIDEBOOK TO MENTAL TOUGHNESS TRAINING FOR MARATHON RUNNERS:

PEAK PERFORMANCE THROUGH MEDITATION, CALMNESS OF MIND, AND STRESS MANAGEMENT

By

Joseph Correa

Certified Meditation Instructor

Introduction

The Beginners Guidebook to Mental Toughness Training for Marathon Runners will teach you how meditation can make you mentally tougher even in the most challenging conditions. Stimulating the mind will stimulate the body to overcome what was once thought of as impossible and will help you surpass limits you never imagined.

Mental road blocks and past mental failures affect what you think you can accomplish but that can be corrected through meditation so that the past stays in the past and you can finally move forward in achieving your goals.

Meditation can become the fastest path to mental toughness due to the non-physical skills you will develop and improve. It will teach you to strengthen the mind and sharpen your concentration for longer periods of time. Give yourself the opportunity to become better in every way imaginable and reach for the top!

What is meditation?

Meditation is a state of mind where you are thinking about something in a calm and relaxed manner. Normally, you are achieving a much higher state of focus.

How will you benefit from meditating?

Meditation will take you to the next level mentally, physically, and emotionally. You can expect to feel more prepared, relaxed, and focused than ever before after meditating. Remember, the body can only do what the mind thinks it can do.

What Improvements can I expect from practicing meditation?

Some of the improvements you can expect are: fewer or no headaches at all, improved digestion, more energy during the day, less muscle cramps or signs of muscle tightness, increased capacity to concentrate over long periods of time.

Does my nutrition affect my meditative potential and is a nutrition plan included?

Yes, nutrition is a major component in becoming mentally tougher. When you have the energy and mental balance needed, you can perform at your optimal mental capacity and this means eating and staying hydrated. Feeling tired, anxious, drowsy, or sleepy will not allow you to focus and perform properly. A meal calendar is included as well as recipes you can use to maximize your meditation sessions and have an organized nutrition.

Chapter 1:

What Is Meditation and How Will Meditation Make You Mentally Tougher?

Basically, meditation is a state of mind where you are reflecting or thinking about something with a calm mind. Meditation and normal thinking are two different things. When meditating you are achieving a much higher state of concentration where nothing is clouding your mind and interacting with your thoughts.

Mediation requires much more concentration and that's why it's so important to be in a distraction free environment where external noises won't interrupt your focus.

Your normal thoughts may last for a few seconds but in meditation those thoughts and the relaxation process is meant to last from 5 minutes to however long you want.

Thoughts can be many but when meditating you hyper focus on one thought at a time. Sometimes when meditating you might just focus on having a clear mental state.

Meditation can be used for religious or non-religious purposes but in this book it will be used for non-religious purposes only.

You can use meditation at any time during the day or at night when you feel you need to calm yourself down and find a state of feeling more mentally balanced.

As you become more advanced at meditation you will move into this state of mind quicker because you will get better at blocking out distractions, and this will allow you to center your mind much sooner.

In meditation you want to zone out negative interfering thoughts, stressful situations, or any interrupting factors when you're trying to reach a state of much higher and deeper focus on any ideas you are working to concentrate on.

To maximize your potential you will need to be able to quiet the mind and leave any mental distractions behind and let your mind surpass any obstacles in the way.

Meditation as exercise for the mind helps to strengthen your mind as you would strengthen your body, consistently evolving as you practice it.

Physical conditioning, good nutrition, and meditation are the three keys to achieve a state of optimal performance. Most marathon runners don't pay as much attention to meditation as they should because their mostly worried about appearance and how others perceive them.

Results, in meditation, are not something you will see physically but rather in how you feel and in your new ability to control your thoughts and emotions. By starting your meditation sessions and being disciplined and consistent you will notice significant improvements in how you respond to anxiety, pressure, and stress which are three of the major issues most marathon runners have trouble overcoming in life and when trying to reach their true potential.

How Will Meditation Make You Mentally Tougher?

The benefits of meditation can be broken down to physical benefits, mental benefits, and emotional benefits. Mental Toughness is a result of overcoming mental obstacles and meditation teaches you to stay calm and find solutions even under pressure.

It doesn't matter if you are tall, short, smart, or slow, meditation is for anyone who wants to improve themselves.

I find that emotionally, meditation is wonderful but everyone is different and you might find it to benefit one aspect of your life more than others.

Meditation has been shown to help anxiety, reduction and since anxiety and stress are some of the most serious mental issues affecting marathon runners around the world, this is an important topic. Meditation prevents overall progress of stress and anxiety to better overcome it and eliminate it as much as possible from our lives.

In fact, meditation is on the best ways to control stress and reduce health problems that arise due to stress. Stress can cause lack of sleep and a reduction of energy levels which will affect your attitude, performance at work, patience, and tolerance.

Meditation is one of the greatest stress controlling techniques around, so you can easily start adding it to your life and begin feeling healthier and better on a day to day basis.

Physical Benefits

When most athletes think of something granting physical benefits, their thoughts tend to be on some form of physical exercise. This might include exercises like: running, biking, swimming, walking, and weight training. It's normal to think of physical exercises as a solution to improve your physical health but physical benefits can come about in different ways and meditation proves this.

Some of the physical improvements that can be seen after meditating are:

1. **Your ability to reduce your heart rate** to help you control your emotions better. Stress and anxiety have a tendency to increase your heart rate. Being able to control this will be very beneficial if you're under pressure constantly.

2. **Your ability to reduce your blood pressure.** Besides lowing your heart rate, meditation will also help you with lowing your blood pressure. High blood pressure levels equate to a much greater risk of heart disease and stroke. Too many things in our environment, especially food, easily raise your blood pressure. Having a powerful tool like meditation on your side will assist you in overcoming this.

3. **Your ability to control muscular tension.** Marathon runners who have tight muscles usually will be more prone to muscular imbalances and can have muscle tears much

more often than people who have learned to relax their muscles. Marathon runners will recover much faster and feel less fatigued after meditating. When you reduce muscle tension, your muscles will recover faster due to the improved quality of rest which will only improve physical performance. For marathon runners who compete at high levels, you don't want to overlook this benefit.

4. **Your ability to stay calm under stressful situations.** Being able to control your emotions better will help you to stay calm when things don't go the way you planned them to or when things get stressful.

5. **Your improved approach towards anxiety and fear.** Most marathon runners find themselves worrying less and being less afraid to do things after they have been able to think things through in their mind first. This will better prepare you and make you feel more confident.

6. **Your ability to strengthen your immune system.** Being less stressed out, less worried, having lower blood pressure levels, and resting better will all account for an improved immune system that will help you feel stronger, healthier, and more energetic than ever before.

7. **Enhanced ability to recover after physical training.** Meditation can help to strengthen the immune system response time, and this in turn can help you recover faster from workout sessions that you are doing. If your immune system, is weak, as is normal for become who are constantly under pressure, in a rush, and seriously stressed out, this can make you feel tired which makes it harder to bounce back after a workout session is completed. By practicing meditation on a daily basis, you will see a faster increase in your rate of recovery so that you can be ready sooner and get back to training again with more energy.

These were some of the most common physical benefits that you will see and feel from practicing meditation. You will notice meditation requires little or no movement at all, but don't think that it won't influence you in a physical way.

Mental Toughness

As you can imagine, the mental or psychological benefits of meditation tend to be even more powerful as this is largely a mentally-focused form of practice.

Some of the primary aspects of meditation that will increase your mental toughness are:

1. **Improved approach towards anger.** Some marathon runners tend to get angry very easily, sometimes for no reason at all. The first mental benefit you will see is a reduced level of anger and aggression. Because you will feel more in control over your emotions. You will be less likely to let your emotions get the best of you. For those that tend to be very aggressive on a daily basis, you can use

meditation to calm these feelings down when they start to get out of hand.

2. **Improved capacity to concentrate.** Meditation can help you to focus for much longer periods of time and will allow you to make these, high quality concentration periods. THIS IS ONE OF THE GREATEST BENEFITS YOU CAN OBTAIN FROM MEDITATING and one that should not be overlooked. Being able to block out distractions and stay focused on the task at hand can be a major obstacle that meditation will help you overcome.

3. **Greater confidence in yourself.** Most marathon runners who regularly perform meditation often say they feel more confident. Self-confidence comes from feeling you have greater control over specific events in your life. When you have more self-esteem, it will show in everything you do, whether it's interacting with others or when trying to reach your goals. Meditation can

make you feel empowered and strong. For most athletes, the reduction in stress alone is enough motivation to keep them practicing meditation on a daily basis.

4. **You'll feel more relaxed.** The process of breathing and closing your eyes combined with focused thinking will help you feel calmer and more relaxed.

How Can Marathon Runners Benefit?

Marathon runners can benefit from meditation by seeing a faster rate of recovery which is fundamental when trying to push yourself to the next level of performance. Training sessions will be more intense and of higher quality due to the improved level of concentration and due to the reduction of fatigue in their muscles. Most marathon runners will see a reduction in nervousness before and during competition which will help them compete better and more confidently.

Once you start practicing on a regular basis you will find that you have increased capacity to concentrate and focus, when it comes time to perform under pressure and under unexpected conditions. This increased capacity to focus will take you to an even higher level of performance.

Marathon runners with risk of heart disease can benefit significantly from meditation. Doctors are now prescribing more meditation and less medication which is common sense for some and life changing for others. By simply reducing the amount of stress a marathon runner is exposed to on a daily basis will reduce blood pressure levels and improve their competitiveness by being able to take on more training. Some marathon runners have found that meditation can often help control stress eating which is not commonly talked about but a significant factor that steers people away from reaching their peak performance. Marathon runners often find they are more in control of their lives after repeating meditation sessions often which reduces stress and as a direct benefit, lowers the risk of heart disease.

Weight loss is a common problem because of not having proper planning and not being able to follow diets because of lack of discipline or poor habits. MEDITATION CAN ACTUALLY HELP WITH WEIGHT LOSS TO HAPPEN when overeating is due to stress.

Marathon runners trying to break bad habits will find it difficult to change their old ways and start on a new path. Smoking, drinking alcohol, nervousness, getting angry, and other negative habits can be controlled through meditation as it can reduce cravings. Slowing things down and using breathing techniques to focus on overcoming bad habits when meditating can be a powerful technique that seems less obvious but more relevant when bad habits have been developed due to stress and anger.

Marathon runners who suffer from depression or anxiety also suffer from stress as it is a major contributor towards the first two. Negative health states can be dramatically improved through the practice of meditation on a regular basis. When you practicing meditation you will notice it easier for you to have more control over your mood and will feel more positive about the future in general. Many marathon runners worry too much about the outcome or past failed outcomes which are irrelevant to the present if you take the time to maximize your present potential through improved nutrition and meditation. If your goal is to control your thoughts and emotions better, you will find that meditating will calm you down and allow you not to feel overwhelmed under strenuous situations.

Chapter 2:

Common Forms of Meditation for

Marathon Runners

Mindfulness

During mindfulness, marathon runners should be trying to stay in the present in each and every thought that they currently have entering their mind.

This type of meditation teaches you to become aware of your breathing patterns, but doesn't attempt to change them in any way through breathing practices.

This is a more passive form of meditation compared to other more active forms of meditation which will require you to change your breathing patterns.

Mindfulness is one of the most common types of meditation in the world and one that all athletes can greatly benefit from.

Focused meditation

Marathon runners using meditation are directing their thoughts to a specific problem, emotion, or object they want to focus on and find a solution for.

Begin by clearing your mind of all distractions and then taking some time to focus on just a single sound, object, or thought. You are trying to focus for as long as possible in this state of mind where you can then redirect your concentration to an objective you want to achieve.

It's your choice if you want to move on to work on any other objective or thought, or you can also just maintain that initial focus on the sound, object, or thought you first had.

Movement meditation

Movement meditation is another form of meditation you should try as well. This is a type of meditation where you focus on your breathing patterns, moving the air into and out of your lungs, while doing flowing movement patterns (with your hands) which you will repeat. You might feel uncomfortable at the beginning by moving with your eyes closed but with time you will notice it is actually very relaxing and will help you to improve your overall health.

A mind to body connection will be optimized in this type of meditation, especially for people who have trouble staying still and prefer to move around in a natural flowing motion. These movements should be slow and repetitive. The more controlled they are, the better. Doing fast, or violent movements will undo the benefit of meditating.

People who practice yoga often find this form of meditation great as it is a good compliment and similar to yoga breathing and movement exercises. Both improve control over yourself and over thoughts. For people who have never done yoga before and have already done movement meditation, will find that warming up with some yoga based exercises can often help you ease into movement meditation faster. The goal is to enter a meditative state quicker and yoga will definitely allow you to do this in a natural way. While yoga focuses more on improving flexibility and developing muscle strength, movement meditation is directed more towards a mental state and slow breathing patterns.

Mantra meditation

Mantra meditation is going to help you focus better on your thoughts and clear your mind to maximize the effect of meditating.

During mantra meditation you will be citing mantras over and over as you follow your meditative process.

A mantra could be a sound, phrase, or prayer that's chanted over and over.

We will not be focusing on spiritual meditation but it is another type of meditation besides focused meditation, mindfulness, mantra meditation, and movement meditation.

Everyone is different which means you don't have to use just one type of meditation to achieve your goals. You can use one or more forms of meditation and in different order.

Chapter 3:

Prepare to Succeed

Once you know what type of meditation you will be doing, you need to know how to prepare to meditate. Make sure not to rush through your meditation process as this will certainly reduce the overall effects and diminish possible results.

EQUIPMENT: Place a mat, blanket, towel, or chair where you plan to meditate.

Some people prefer to use a towel (which is great when you are traveling or out of town), or a mat to sit on or lay flat on your back on. Others prefer to sit on a chair to have a stable position that will help you not to fall asleep if you feel too relaxed.

I prefer to sit on a yoga mat as it is a position that I feel helps me focus and relax. Sometimes I warm up with yoga or static stretching so I will already have my mat ready but when I travel I simply use a thick towel.

Being comfortable is very important to get in the right state of mind so make sure you use the right equipment to get started.

TIME: Decide how long you will meditate for in advance

Make sure you decide beforehand for how long you plan on meditating and with what purpose.

For something simple like focusing on being positive and breathing, you can plan on doing a short session of about 5 to 15 minutes long. Whereas if you plan on focusing on a problem and want to try and find a solution for, you might want to plan on giving yourself enough time to first relax through breathing patterns and then start to focus on alternative solutions to the problem at hand.

This might take anywhere from 10 minutes to an hour or longer depending on your level of experience in meditating or it may also depend on how long it takes you to get in a relaxed state of mind that will allow you to focus well enough to confront the problem.

Plan on how long you will take so that you can prepare beforehand to stay at the same location until you're done without interruptions such as: being hungry, kids coming into the room, bathroom breaks, etc. Take care of these possible distractions beforehand.

LOCATION: Finding a clean, quiet, and comfortable space to meditate

Find a place where you can totally relax and clear your mind with no interruptions.

This can be anywhere you feel comfortable and can reach this relaxed state of mind. It could be on the grass in a park, at home in your room, in your bathroom, in a quiet empty room, or by yourself in your car. This is completely up to you.

Make sure your cell phone is off. It's impossible to get the results you want from meditating by having constant distractions and now a days cell phones are a main source of distraction and interruptions.

The location you choose should have these things in common: it should be quiet, clean, and needs to be at a cool room temperature (too warm will put you to sleep and too cold will make you want to get up and move around), it should be clear of distractions.

PREPARATION: Prepare your body to meditate

Before meditating make sure you do whatever you need to do to get your body relaxed and ready. This could be by taking a shower, stretching, putting on comfortable clothes, etc.

Make sure you eat at least 30 minutes before starting so that you don't feel hungry or too full. A lean meal would be ideal to help you prepare properly beforehand. I will go into more depth on the importance of nutrition in one of the following chapters.

WARM UP: Do some Yoga or stretch beforehand to start relaxing.

For some of you who have already done yoga in the past, know how relaxing it can be. Those of you who have not started doing yoga, it would be a good time to start since it will help you to better relax and calm yourself down. It's not necessary to do yoga before meditating but it helps in order to maximize the effects and speed up the relaxing process to get you in the right state of mind. Stretching is another good alternative since stretching combined with some breathing exercises will help you calm down and feel more at ease.

MENTALITY: Do some deep breathing to start calming yourself down

Breathing is easy but practicing breathing takes more time. The benefits of practicing breathing techniques are many.

Most marathon runners will find themselves recovering faster after intense moments. They will also notice they are able to stay focused even when out of breath. Marathon runners need to focus on the air moving into and out of their lungs, pay attention to how the body expands and contracts. Hearing and feeling the air move in and out of your nose and mouth will help you feel more relaxed and is the proper to focus on your breathing. Every time you breathe in and is then exhaled try to focus on going into a deeper and deeper state of relaxation. Every time oxygen fills your lungs your body will feel more energized and full of positive emotions.

ENVIRONMENT: Add some meditative or relaxing music in the background only if it does not become a distraction.

If meditation music helps you get into a relaxed state, by all means include it in your meditation session. Everything and anything that helps you get into a more focused and relaxed state should be used, including music.

If you feel you are able to clear your mind better without any sounds or music, then don't add music to your environment.

I normally don't add music simply because I find music takes me in other directions which I don't always want to go since some music reminds me of other thoughts and ideas. That's just me but maybe music is right for you. Try both options to see what works better for you. Some marathon runners like to listen to music before competing since they feel it relaxes them or gets them in the right mood. Find what works for you and stick to it.

Common Meditative Positions

When it comes to meditating positions it's basically up to you. There is no wrong or right position, only the one that gets you in the best state of concentration. For some people sitting on a chair is great because of the back support, while others prefer to be closer to the ground and will decide to sit on a towel.

For people who are less flexible the lotus position might be something you may want to skip or wait to try out as it might feel too uncomfortable to hold for a long period of time. Again, make sure you can stay in the same position for the time period you are planning to meditate for or else choose another position.

Sitting position

For the sitting position simply find a chair that you feel will allow you to focus without making you feel too uncomfortable or that relaxes you too much where you feel sleepy. Make sure your back is straight when seated and that your feet can touch the floor as you don't want to finish your meditation session with back pain. Some people prefer to add a soft pillow to their chair to feel more comfortable.

Kneeling on the floor

Take your shoes and socks off if you want to and kneel on the ground. Try kneeling on top of a soft mat or folded towel as to have your toes pointing behind you and your hips directly above your heels. Your back should be straight and relaxed as to allow your lungs to expand and contract as much times as necessary. You want to create a strong connection through your breathing and to do this, air has to go in and out of your lungs in a flowing motion.

Burmese position

The Burmese position is similar to a butterfly stretching position but with a change in the position of the feet. Sit down on the floor and open your legs, then bend your knees while bringing your feet towards the inside part of your legs. One foot should be in front of the other. When in this position try to keep your knees down as low as possible. If it feels uncomfortable choose another position as there are many options. Your hands should be at your sides or together in a finger crossing-over position. Your back should be straight and your forehead tilting slightly up and forward to allow you to take in air and release it in a full and complete manner. This is an advanced meditation position so it's not necessary to start with it unless you feel completely relaxed in it.

Lotus position

The Lotus position is very similar to the Burmese position but with a small alteration. You will need to bring your feet on top of your thighs while in a

Burmese position. Your hands should be at your sides or together in a finger crossing-over position.

My knees feel uncomfortable in this position so I don't use it for my meditation sessions but you are free to try it as long as it does not cause pain. You don't want the pain you feel to take all your attention from your goal of focused breathing and calmness. If you don't like this position, simply choose another.

Laying down position

Lay down on the mat, towel, or blanket and relax your feet and hands. Your hands should stay at your sides and your feet pointing up or outwards. Your hands can be placed on your stomach in a gentle but still position or at your sides. Your head needs to stay facing the ceiling or the sky. If you tilt it to one side or another, this will not allow you to stay focused for long periods of time and might even end up with some neck tension. This is a great position to meditate in (when done correctly) as long as you don't fall asleep. If this is your problem, simply choose another position.

Butterfly position

In this position you will need to sit down on your mat or towel, open your legs and then bring your feet together so that the bottom of each is facing one another. Your knees might flare upwards or they might be able to go down to the ground, it does not matter as long as you feel comfortable and can relax in this position. Make sure your spine is straight and balanced.

Chapter 4:

Performance Enhancing Breathing Patterns for Improved Mental Toughness

Performance enhancing breathing patterns will be the key to set the pace of your meditation session and also to get into a hyper focused state.

For the mindfulness form of mediation you will continue to stay concentrated but you want to be more aware of your breathing. Your goal should not be to control your breathing but to simply feel the air going into your lungs and then out to your surroundings. The breathing in and out process should be done only through the nose for this specific type of meditation but should not be used for the other forms of meditation.

For the remainder of the other meditation types, you want to pay attention to breathing patterns and direct them through your session. All breathing patterns should be done by breathing in through your nose and out through your mouth (except when doing mindfulness meditation).

In order to get into a better meditative state, your heart rate needs to drop and to do this, breathing will be essential. The patterns you use will facilitate this process to help you reach higher levels of concentration.

With practice these breathing patterns will become second nature to you. Decide beforehand if slow breathing patterns are better for you or if fast breathing patterns will be what you need. Slow breathing patterns relax you and fast breathing patterns energize you.

SLOW BREATHING PATTERNS

In order to slow down your breathing you will want to take in air slowly and for a longer period of time and then release it slowly as well. For marathon runners, this type of breathing is good to get you to relax after training or about an hour before competition.

Different ratios of air in and air out will affect your level of relaxation, and in turn your ability to reach an optimal level of meditation.

Normal slow breathing pattern: Start by taking air in through your nose slowly and counting to 5. Then, release slowly counting back down from 5 to 1. You should repeat this process 4 to 10 times until you feel completely relaxed and ready to focus. Marathon runners should focus on breathing in through the nose and out through the mouth for this type of breathing pattern.

Extended slow breathing pattern: Start by taking air in through your nose slowly and counting to 7. Then, release slowly counting back down from 7 to 1 while exhaling out through your mouth. You should repeat this process 4 to 6 times until you feel completely relaxed and ready to focus.

Slow breathing pattern for hyperactive marathon runners: Start by taking air in through your nose slowly and counting to 3. Then, release slowly counting back down from 6 to 1 while exhaling out through your mouth. You should repeat this process 4 to 6 times until you feel relaxed and ready to focus. This pattern will force you to slow down completely. The last repetition of this sequence should end with 4 seconds in and 4 seconds out to stabilize your breathing.

Ultra-slow breathing pattern: Begin by taking air in through your nose slowly and counting to 4. Then, release slowly counting back down from 10 to 1 while exhaling out through your mouth. You should repeat this process 4 to 6 times until you feel completely relaxed and ready to meditate. This pattern will force you to slow down gradually. The last 2 repetitions of this sequence should end with 4 seconds in and 4 seconds out to stabilize your breathing and balance the air in and out ratio.

Stabilizing breathing patterns before meditating: This is a good type of breathing pattern that should be used if you feel you are already calm and want to start immediately meditating. Start by taking air in through your nose slowly and counting to 3. Then, release slowly counting back down from 3 to 1. You should repeat this process 7 to 10 times until you feel completely relaxed and ready to focus. Marathon runners should focus on breathing in through the nose and out through the mouth for this type of breathing pattern.

FAST BREATHING PATTERNS

Fast breathing patterns are very important for marathon runners in order to get energized and ready to compete. Even though this type of breathing pattern is most effective when visualizing, it will be just as useful for meditating. For marathon runners that are very calm and need to feel more in control of their mind might want to use these patterns to get themselves ready to meditate.

Normal fast breathing pattern: Start by taking air in through your nose slowly and counting to 5. Then, release slowly counting back down from 3 to

1. You should repeat this process 6 to 10 times until you feel completely relaxed and ready to meditate. Marathon runners should focus on breathing in through the nose and out through the mouth for this type of breathing pattern.

Prolonged fast breathing pattern: Start by taking air in through your nose slowly and counting to 10. Then, release slowly counting back down from 5 to 1 while exhaling out through your mouth. You should repeat this process 5 to 6 times until you feel completely relaxed. If you have trouble getting to 10 at first, simply lower the count to 7 or 8. Focus on breathing in through the nose and out through the mouth.

Pre-competition fast breathing pattern: Start by taking air in through your nose slowly and counting to 6. Then, release quickly in one breath while exhaling out through your mouth. You should repeat this process 5 to 6 times until you feel completely relaxed and ready to focus. You can add 2 repetitions to this sequence with 4 seconds in and 4 seconds out to stabilize your breathing and balance the air in and out ratio.

All of these types of breathing patterns are performance enhancing and can be used during competition depending on your level of energy or nervousness.

For marathon runners that get nervous before competition you should use slow breathing patterns.

For marathon runners that need to get energized before competition you should use the fast breathing patterns.

In case of anxiety, a combination of slow breathing patterns followed by fast breathing patterns will give you optimal results.

During training sessions or during competition when feeling exhausted or out of breath use the normal fast breath breathing pattern to help recover quicker.

Breathing patterns are a great way to control your levels of intensity which in turn will save you energy and allow you to recover faster.

Chapter 5:

Mental Toughness Nutrition Calendar for Marathon Runners

Mental Toughness is the end goal to better yourself and proper nutrition will help you reach this goal. Eating right equates to having more energy and for extended periods of time.

This in turn affects your capacity to stay focused for prolonged time periods. Lean proteins, omega fats, vegetables and legumes, and water are the best pre-meditation foods and should be eaten in appropriate amounts depending on your caloric needs.

Having too much sugar in your blood stream will force you to crash before, during, or after meditating and the same will happen in competition so refined sugars are not the way to go. Avoid large meals that might make you feel too full and will make you want to stop meditating or put you to sleep.

Meals that are too small will make you hungry too soon which will shorten your meditation sessions and not allow you to maximize results.

Eating 60-75 minutes before meditating will give you more than sufficient time to digest and be ready to meditate properly.

Hydrating properly is essential as well and should be taken seriously. Drink at least 8 glasses of water a day and make sure you are getting enough vitamins and minerals as to not dehydrate.

Mental Toughness Nutrition Calendar

DAY	BREAKFAST	SNACK	LUNCH	SNACK	DINNER
1.	2 boiled eggs with chopped basil	1 grapefruit	1 beef sirloin with slices of eggplant	1 cup of tomato and walnuts salad	1 cup of cooked chard with olive oil
2.	½ cup of baked mushrooms with rosemary	1 pear	1 cup of octopus salad with tomatoes and capers	1 cup of roasted almonds	1 grilled zucchini with garlic and parsley
3.	1 glass of mixed fruits and vegetables shake	1 glass of fresh apricot juice	2 cups of fish stew	1 peach	1 cup of fresh fruits of your choice
4.	½ cup of pineapple omelette with almonds	1 orange	1 beef chop with pineapple and tumeric	1 cup of chopped cucumber with fennel	2 apples
5.	1 cup of fruit salad	1 cup of tuna salad with lettuce and curry	1 turkey drumstick with nutmeg and carob	3 grilled eggplant slices with chopped fennel	1 cup of octopus salad with tomatoes and capers
6.	1 cup of spinach omelet	1 glass of fresh pineapple juice without sugar	1 medium piece of eggplant casserole	1 cup of cooked leek with lemon sauce	2 boiled eggs with grated ginger
7.	1 cup of tomato and walnuts salad	1 cup of cooked mushrooms with vegetables and ginger sauce	3 chicken wings with tumeric sauce	1 cup of tomato and tuna salad	1 veal steak with red pepper sauce
8.	½ cup of mushroom omelet	1 glass of fresh cranberry juice	2 turkey fillet with walnuts and maple syrup	2 boiled eggs	1 cup of roasted cherry tomatoes, eggplant and basil salad

9.	½ cup of nutmeg omelet	1 cup of shrimps in tomato sauce	1 cup of lettuce salad	5 dried plums	1 cup of coriander salad
10.	2 fried eggs with chopped mint	1 cup of tuna salad with lettuce and curry	1 veal chop with chopped cloves	1 cup of tomato soup	2 boiled eggs with chopped coriander
11.	3 pineapple slices with grated almonds	1 grilled zucchini with chopped basil and mint	1 cup of chopped veal soup with vegetables	2 cooked carrots	1 cup of grapes
12.	1 cup of cooked broccoli	2 cups of fruit salad	1 lamb cutlet with hazelnut sauce	1 grilled red pepper	1 cooked potato in parsley sauce
13.	1 cup of eggplant pate	1 cup of lettuce and tuna salad	½ cup of stewed beef and cabbage	1 cup of broccoli soup	1 cup of roasted almonds
14.	1 glass of fresh orange juice	½ cup of walnuts	1 grilled trout fillets with parsley	1 cup of fresh cranberries and grated walnuts	1 cup of cauliflower soup
15.	½ cup of tomato omelet	1 cup of berries	1 grilled salmon fillet	2 carrots	1 cup of roasted almonds
16.	1 glass of fresh orange and lime juice	1 cup of mixed vegetable salad	1 cup of grilled calamari in curry sauce	3 fresh figs	2 grilled sardines
17.	1 glass of banana shake	2 grilled green peppers	1 cup of seafood salad	2 baked apples	1 grilled zucchini with garlic
18.	2 boiled eggs	1 pear and roasted almonds	1 grilled steak with pineapple slices	1 cup of cooked cauliflower in mint sauce	1 grated apple with walnuts and cinnamon
19.	1 cup of mushroom soup	1 trout fillet with almond and tumeric sauce	1 cup of trout soup	1 cup of cucumber salad	½ cup of grilled mushrooms with garlic sauce
20.	1 glass of fresh lime juice	2 cups of cooked, canned broccoli	1 beef chop with pineapple and tumeric	1 glass of fresh tomato juice	2 grilled sardines

21.	3 apple and carrot balls with cinnamon	1 grilled eggplant with parsley	1 cup of steak salad with mushrooms	1 cooked carrot	1 sour asparagus
22.	1 glass of fruit shake	3 grilled eggplant slices	1 veal cutlet with almonds	1 cup of berries and Brazil nuts	2 grilled red peppers
23.	½ cup of spinach omelet	1 cup tomato and garlic soup	2 squids stuffed with walnuts	1 glass of fresh lemonade	½ cup of Brazil nuts
24.	1 banana	1 cup of lettuce and tuna salad	1 lamb cutlet with basil	1 cucumber	1 cup of grilled mushrooms in tomato sauce
25.	2 fried eggs	½ cup of Brazil and Macadamia nuts	1 cup of shrimp skewers	1 cup of cooked broccoli	1 glass of fresh vegetable juice of your choice
26.	3 pineapple slices with grated almonds	1 cup of broccoli soup	2 turkey fillet with walnuts and maple syrup salmon in almond sauce	1 cup of lettuce and cherry tomato salad	1 apple
27.	1 glass of fresh carrot juice	1 cup of cucumber salad	1 beef chop with pineapple and tumeric	1 cup of chopped cucumber with fennel	1 cup of cooked leek with lemon sauce
28.	1 cup of tomato and walnuts salad	1 glass of fresh apricot juice	2 cups of fish stew	3 dried plums	1 cup of trout soup
29.	3 apple and carrot balls with cinnamon	1 grilled zucchini with chopped basil and mint	1 beef chop with pineapple and tumeric	1 cup of roasted almonds	1 cup of octopus salad with tomatoes and capers
30.	1 cup of eggplant pate	1 cup of cooked mushrooms with vegetables and ginger sauce	1 medium piece of eggplant casserole	1 glass of lemonade without sugar	1 cup of roasted cherry tomatoes, eggplant and basil salad

Chapter 6:

Mental Toughness Nutrition Recipes for Marathon Runners

1. Boiled eggs with chopped basil

Ingredients:

2 eggs

1 tsp of chopped basil

pepper

Preparation:

Boil eggs for 10 minutes. Peel and chop into small pieces. Sprinkle with chopped basil.

Nutritional values per 100 g:

Carbohydrates 1.1g

Sugar 0g

Protein 13g

Total fat (good monounsaturated fat) 11g

Sodium 124mg

Potassium 126mg

Calcium 50mg

Iron 1.2mg

Vitamins (vitamin A; B-6; B-12; C)

Calories 155

2. Beef sirloin with slices of eggplant

Ingredients:

1 thin beef sirloin

1 medium eggplant

1 tsp of olive oil

chopped basil

pepper

Preparation:

Wash and pepper the meat. Grill it on a barbecue pan for about 10 minutes on each side. Remove from pan. Peel eggplant and cut two thick slices. Fry for few minutes in the same barbecue pan. Remove from heat and serve with beef. Sprinkle with chopped basil.

Nutritional values:

Carbohydrates 6g

Sugar 1.2g

Protein 35.2 g

Total fat 4.9g

Sodium 57 mg

Potassium 397mg

Calcium 18.5mg

Iron 1.9mg

Vitamins (vitamin A; B-6; B-12; C; D; D2; D3; K;Thiamin; K)

Calories 212

3. Tomato and walnuts salad

Ingredients:

1 big tomato

½ cup of chopped walnuts

1 tsp of lemon juice

Preparation:

Wash and cut tomato into small pieces. Add chopped walnuts and mix well. Pour lemon juice over it.

Nutritional values for 1 cup:

Carbohydrates 8.2g

Sugar 3.8g

Protein 10g

Total fat 4.5g

Sodium 17 mg

Potassium 112mg

Calcium 16.5mg

Iron 1.3mg

Vitamins (vitamin A; B-6; B-12; C; D; D2; D3; K; Riboflavin; Niacin; Thiamin; K)

Calories 218

4. Cooked chard with olive oil

Ingredients:

1 bunch of chard

1 tsp of olive oil

1 tsp of tumeric

Preparation:

Wash and chop chard. Fry it in olive oil for 20 minutes on a low temperature, or until tender. Add tumeric before serving.

Nutritional values for one cup:

Carbohydrates 6.9g

Sugar 2.1g

Protein 8.4 g

Total fat 1.9g

Sodium 34.2 mg

Potassium 23.2mg

Calcium 12.4mg

Iron 0.59mg

Vitamins (vitamin A; B-6; B-12; C; D; D2; D3; K; Riboflavin; Niacin; Thiamin; K)

Calories 113

5. Baked mushrooms with rosemary

Ingredients:

1 cup of mushrooms

1 tsp of olive oil

1 tsp of chopped rosemary

Preparation:

Bake mushrooms in a barbecue pan for 5-7 minutes. Remove from pan and sprinkle with olive oil and chopped rosemary.

Nutritional values for one cup:

Carbohydrates 6.2g

Sugar 1.1g

Protein 8.4 g

Total fat (good monounsaturated fat) 1.3g

Sodium 48.2 mg

Potassium 23.2mg

Calcium 12.4mg

Iron 0.59mg

Vitamins (vitamin A; B-6; B-12; C; D; D2; D3; K; Riboflavin; Niacin; Thiamin; K)

Calories 117

6. Octopus salad with tomatoes and capers

Ingredients:

1 cup of frozen cut octopus

¼ cup of capers

½ cup of olives

5 cherry tomatoes

1 tsp of chopped parsley

1 tsp of chopped celery

1 small onion

2 cloves of garlic

1 tsp of chopped rosemary

1 tbsp of olive oil

1 tsp of lemon juice

Preparation:

Cook the octopus in salted water until tender. It usually takes about 20-30 minutes. Remove from pot, wash and drain. Wash and cut vegetables and mix with octopus. Mix the spices and add to salad. Sprinkle with olive oil and lemon juice. Cool well before serving.

Nutritional values for one cup:

Carbohydrates 12.9g

Sugar 5.1g

Protein 16.4 g

Total fat (good monounsaturated fat) 9.9g

Sodium 114.2 mg

Potassium 83.2mg

Calcium 42.4mg

Iron 0.59mg

Vitamins (vitamin A; B-6; B-12; C; D; D2; D3; K; Riboflavin; Niacin; Thiamin; K)

Calories 81

7. Grilled zucchini with garlic and parsley

Ingredients:

1 medium zucchini

1 tbsp of chopped parsley

2 cloves of garlic

Preparation:

Peel the zucchini and cut into 4 slices. Fry in a barbecue pan for 3-4 minutes. Add chopped garlic and bake for another 5 minutes. Sprinkle with parsley before serving.

Nutritional values:

Carbohydrates 3.71g

Sugar 3g

Protein 2 g

Total fat 0g

Sodium 2.9 mg

Potassium 360mg

Calcium 0.2mg

Iron 0.3mg

Vitamins (vitamin A; B-6; B-12; C; D:K)

Calories 20

8. Mixed fruits and vegetables shake

Ingredients:

1 cup of mixed blueberries, raspberries, blackberries and strawberries

½ cup of chopped baby spinach

2 cups of water

Preparation:

Mix ingredients in a blender for few minutes.

Nutritional values for 1 cup:

Carbohydrates 9.2g

Sugar 6.15g

Protein 8.75g

Total fat 0.87g

Sodium 54.8mg

Potassium 107.8mg

Calcium 82mg

Iron 2.03mg

Vitamins (Vitamin C total ascorbic acid; B-6; B-12; Folate-DFE; A-RAE; A-IU; E-alpha-tocopherol; D; D-D2+D3; K-phylloquinone; Thianin; Riboflavin; Niacin)

Calories 42.6

9. Fish stew

Ingredients:

1 carp fillet

1 carrot

2 chili peppers

1 medium tomato

pepper

celery roots and leaf

Preparation:

It is the best to buy cooked carrots, or cook them before preparing the fish stew. Wash and cut vegetables, mix with celery and fish and put in a pot. Pour little water, just to cover it. Cook on a low temperature for 20-30 minutes.

Nutritional values:

Carbohydrates 8.2g

Sugar 3.9g

Protein 15.2 g

Total fat (good monounsaturated fat) 6.6g

Sodium 113.8 mg

Potassium 71mg

Calcium 29.1mg

Iron 0.32mg

Vitamins (vitamin A; B-6; B-12; C; D; D2; D3; K; Riboflavin; Niacin; Thiamin; K)

Calories 172

10. Pineapple omelet with almonds

Ingredients:

3 slices of pineapple

2 eggs

½ cup of almonds

1 tbsp of flaxseed oil for frying

Preparation:

Beat the eggs and add almonds. Fry pineapple slices for few minutes on both sides, without oil. When done, remove from pan, add oil, heat it and add eggs mixture. Serve with baked pineapple slices.

Nutritional values per 100g:

Carbohydrates 8.9g

Sugar 4.6g

Protein 19.2 g

Total fat 13.6g

Sodium 134.8 mg

Potassium 131mg

Calcium 67.1mg

Iron 1.52mg

Vitamins (vitamin A; B-12; C; K; Riboflavin; Niacin; K)

Calories 187

11. Beef chop with pineapple and tumeric

Ingredients:

1 medium beef chop

1 tbsp of olive oil

1 tsp of tumeric

Pepper

2 pineapple slices

Preparation:

Wash and dry the meat. Fry it without oil, in it's own sauce, for 15-20 minutes on low temperature. Remove from heat. Make a sauce with olive oil, tumeric and pepper and spread it over fried beef. Fry it once more for 3-4 minutes, add pineapple slices and serve warm.

Nutritional values per 100g:

Carbohydrates 15.7g

Sugar 9.9g

Protein 34g

Total fat (good monounsaturated fat) 17.6g

Sodium 99.3 mg

Potassium 328mg

Calcium 49.1mg

Iron 0.52mg

Vitamins (vitamin A; B-6; B-12; C; D; D2; D3; K; Riboflavin; Niacin; Thiamin; K)

Calories 311

12. Fruit salad

Ingredients:

1 cup of berries

½ cup of pineapple cubes

½ cup of chopped apple

1 tsp of cinnamon

1 tsp of agave syrup

Preparation:

Mix fruits, add agave syrup and sprinkle with cinnamon.

Nutritional values for one cup:

Carbohydrates 19.2g

Sugar 12g

Protein 15.2 g

Total fat (good monounsaturated fat) 4.6g

Sodium 123.8 mg

Potassium 95mg

Calcium 44.1mg

Iron 0.52mg

Vitamins (vitamin A; B-6; B-12; C; D; D2; D3; K; Riboflavin; Niacin; Thiamin; K)

Calories 77

13. Tuna salad with lettuce and curry

Ingredients:

1 small can of tuna without oil

1 bunch of lettuce

2 chili peppers

1 tsp of curry

1 tsp of lemon sauce

Preparation:

Wash and cut lettuce. Mix it with tuna, add chopped chili peppers and lemon sauce. Sprinkle with curry.

Nutritional values for 1 cup:

Carbohydrates 23.4g

Sugar 13g

Protein 33.2g

Total fat (good monounsaturated fat) 12.4g

Sodium 123mg

Potassium 72.3mg

Calcium 42.1mg

Iron 0.27mg

Vitamins (vitamin A; B-6; B-12; C; D; D2; D3; K; Riboflavin; Niacin; Thiamin; K)

Calories 68

14. Turkey drumstick with nutmeg and carob

Ingredients:

1 turkey drumstick

½ cup of water

½ cup of nutmeg

½ cup of carob

Preparation:

Wash and clean the meat. Fry it for about 15 minutes in it's own sauce (add some water while frying the turkey). Finely chop nutmeg and carob and add to saucepan. Mix well with turkey sauce. Remove from the pan and sprinkle with some more carob.

Nutritional values for one cup:

Carbohydrates 3.2g

Sugar 0.9g

Protein 31g

Total fat (good monounsaturated fat) 10.4g

Sodium 998mg

Potassium 78.2mg

Calcium 48mg

Iron 0.37mg

Vitamins (vitamin A; B-6; B-12; C; D; D2; D3; K; Riboflavin; Niacin; Thiamin; K)

Calories 210

15. Grilled eggplant slices with chopped fennel

Ingredients:

1 large eggplant

½ cup of chopped fennel

1 tbsp of olive oil

1 tsp of chopped parsley

Preparation:

Peel the eggplant and cut into 3 slices. Bake it in a barbecue pan without oil. When done, spread olive oil over it, sprinkle with fennel and parsley.

(These eggplant slices are great cold, so you can leave them overnight in a refrigerator)

Nutritional values per slice:

Carbohydrates 8.9g

Sugar 3g

Protein 7g

Total fat (good monounsaturated fat) 2.4g

Sodium 54mg

Potassium 32.5mg

Calcium 12.4mg

Iron 0.37mg

Vitamins (vitamin A; B-6; B-12; C; D; D2; D3;
K; Riboflavin; Niacin; Thiamin; K)

Calories 54

16. Spinach omelet

Ingredients:

1 cup of chopped spinach

2 eggs

1 tbsp of olive oil for frying

Preparation:

Cook spinach in salted water until tender. Remove from pan and drain. Fry in olive oil for 5-6 minutes and add eggs. Mix well and serve warm.

Nutritional values per 100g:

Carbohydrates 1.9g

Sugar 0.6g

Protein 19.2 g

Total fat 13.6g

Sodium 144mg

Potassium 133mg

Calcium 71mg

Iron 1.8mg

Vitamins (vitamin A; B-12; C; K; Riboflavin; Niacin; K)

Calories 177

17. Eggplant casserole

Ingredients:

2 large eggplants

1 cup of minced meat

1 medium onion

1 tsp of olive oil

pepper

2 medium tomatoes

1 tsp of chopped parsley

Preparation:

Peel the eggplants and cut lengthwise into thin sheets. Put them in a bowl, and leave them to sit for at least an hour. Roll them in beaten eggs. Fry in hot oil. Cut the onion, fry, add sliced peppers, tomato, which is cut into cubes, and finely chopped parsley. Fry for few minutes and then add the meat. When meat is tender, remove from heat, cool, add 1 egg and season with pepper. Put fried eggplant and meat with vegetables in an ovenproof dish and make layers until you have used all the material. Bake for 30 minutes at 300 degrees.

Nutritional values per 100g:

Carbohydrates 7.9g

Sugar 3.4g

Protein 10.2 g

Total fat 13.6g

Sodium 164mg

Potassium 302mg

Calcium 21.1mg

Iron 1.32mg

Vitamins (vitamin A; B-12; C; K; Riboflavin; Niacin; K)

Calories 109

18. Leek with chicken cubes

Ingredients:

2 cups of trimmed leeks

1 cup of chicken fillets, cut into cubes

olive oil

thyme leaves for decoration

salt to taste

Preparation:

Cut the leeks into small pieces and wash it under cold water, day before serving. Leave it overnight in a plastic bag.

Heat the oil in a large pan. Add chicken cubes and fry for about 15 minutes on a medium temperature. Add leaks, mix well and fry for another 10 minutes on a low temperature. Remove from the saucepan and allow it to cool. Decorate with thyme leaves.

Nutritional values for 1 cup:

Carbohydrates 7g

Sugar 1.6g

Protein 18.1 g

Total fat 13.6g

Sodium 124.1 mg

Potassium 120mg

Calcium 69.3mg

Iron 1.42mg

Vitamins (vitamin A; B-6; B-12; C; D; D2; D3; K; Riboflavin; Niacin; Thiamin; K)

Calories 187

19. Cooked mushrooms with vegetables

Ingredients:

2 cups of button mushrooms

1cup of dried turkey cubes

2 large carrots

½ cup of chopped cabbage

1 tsp of ginger

1 tbsp of olive oil

1 tsp of chopped parsley

Preparation:

Cook vegetables in water until tender.
Remove from pan and drain. Allow it to cool
for a while. Mix olive oil, ginger and parsley,
add little water and cook it for few minutes, on
a medium heat. Pour over vegetables, add
dried turkey and mix well. Allow it to cool in
the refrigerator for about 30 minutes before
serving.

Nutritional values for 1 cup:

Carbohydrates 18.6g

Sugar 11.3g

Protein 21.9g

Total fat 14.2g

Sodium 153.3 mg

Potassium 89.8mg

Calcium 49.9mg

Iron 0.42mg

Vitamins (vitamin A; B-6; B-12; C; D; D2; D3; K; Riboflavin; Niacin; Thiamin; K)

Calories 79

20. Chicken wings with tumeric sauce

Ingredients:

2 chicken wings

1 tsp of tumeric

1 tbsp of olive oil

½ tsp of dried rosemary

¼ tsp of red pepper

Preparation:

Fry chicken wings in a barbecue pan for 10-15 minutes. 3-4 minutes before chicken is done, add olive oil, tumeric, rosemary, pepper and a little water. Mix well the sauce and soak the chicken in it.

Nutritional values per 100g:

Carbohydrates 18.6g

Sugar 0.9g

Protein 28g

Total fat 22.7g

Sodium 431.3 mg

Potassium 189mg

Calcium 2.9mg

Iron 2.42mg

Vitamins (vitamin A; B-6; B-12; C; D; D2; D3; K; Riboflavin; Niacin; Thiamin; K)

Calories 318

21. Tomato and tuna salad

Ingredients:

2 large tomatoes

2 medium onions

3 cans of tuna

1 tbsp of olive oil

1 tsp of lemon juice

basil

salt to taste

Preparation:

Wash and peel the vegetables. Cut it into small cubes. Add olive oil, lemon juice and basil. Mix well.

Nutritional values for one cup:

Carbohydrates 17.9g

Sugar 9.1g

Protein 28.3 g

Total fat (good monounsaturated fat) 15.8g

Sodium 127mg

Potassium 89.6mg

Calcium 42.1mg

Iron 0.38mg

Vitamins (vitamin A; B-6; B-12; C; D; D2; D3; K; Riboflavin; Niacin; Thiamin; K)

Calories 99

22. Veal steak with red pepper sauce

Ingredients:

1 medium veal steak

1 large red paprika

1 tsp of red pepper

1 tbsp of olive oil

chopped rosemary

Preparation:

Wash and cut paprika into small pieces. Put in a large pan, add olive oil and rosemary. Stew for 15 minutes on low heat. Add red pepper and cook for another few minutes. Wash and dry the steak. Fry it in a barbecue pan until tender. Add sauce and remove from pan.

Nutritional values per 100g:

Carbohydrates 4.5g

Sugar 2.1g

Protein 26 g

Total fat 9.8g

Sodium 87 mg

Potassium 339mg

Calcium 2.1mg

Iron 0.16mg

Vitamins (vitamin A; B-6; B-12; C; D; D2; D3; K)

Calories 203

23. Mushroom omelet

Ingredients:

1 cup of mushrooms,

2 eggs

1 tbsp of olive oil

Preparation:

Fry the mushrooms in olive oil on a low temperature. Let the mushroom sauce evaporate. Add eggs and mix well.

Nutritional values per 100 g:

Carbohydrates 4.1g

Sugar 0g

Protein 18g

Total fat (good monounsaturated fat) 11g

Sodium 126mg

Potassium 124mg

Calcium 14.9mg

Iron 1.8mg

Vitamins (vitamin A; B-6; B-12; C)

Calories 174

24. Turkey fillet with walnuts and maple syrup

Ingredients:

3 turkey fillets

½ cup of walnuts

1 tsp of maple syrup

¼ cup of water

1 tbsp of olive oil

salt to taste

Preparation:

Fry the fillets in a barbecue pan on a low temperature for about 15 minutes, or until tender. Remove from the heath and add water, maple syrup and walnuts. Mix well and fry for another 5-6 minutes until the water evaporates. Allow it to cool for a while.

Nutritional values per 100 g:

Carbohydrates 10.1g

Sugar 7.3g

Protein 24.2g

Total fat 8.7g

Sodium 1025mg

Potassium 126mg

Calcium 50mg

Iron 1.2mg

Vitamins (vitamin A; B-6; C)

Calories 148

25. Roasted cherry tomatoes, eggplant and basil salad

Ingredients:

1 small eggplant

5 egg whites

1 cup of cherry tomatoes

1 tsp of fresh chopped basil

1 tbsp of olive oil

white pepper to taste

1 tsp of lemon juice

Preparation:

Cut eggplant into thick pieces, dice shape. Salt the eggplant cubes, add oil, egg whites and place on a baking sheet. If necessary, add some more olive oil (this is optional). Bake for about 10 minutes in preheated oven at 350 degrees. Clean the cherry tomatoes and fry for about 15 minutes on a low temperature, using a small saucepan. You want to get lightly caramelized tomato sauce. Remove from the heath and allow it to cool for a while. Gently stir in the lemon sauce, olive oil and fresh basil. Pour over the eggplant and serve cold. A great side dish with barbecue or grilled fish. You can keep it in the fridge up to one week.

Nutritional values per slice:

Carbohydrates 10.4g

Sugar 3g

Protein 19g

Total fat (good monounsaturated fat) 4.9g

Sodium 52mg

Potassium 38.3mg

Calcium 12.9mg

Iron 0.32mg

Vitamins (vitamin A; B-6; B-12; C; D; D2; D3; K; Riboflavin; Niacin; Thiamin; K)

Calories 87

26. Nutmeg omelet

Ingredients:

3 eggs

2 tbsp of olive oil

1 tsp of nutmeg

1/5 tsp of pepper

Preparation:

Beat the eggs and add nutmeg and pepper. Mix well and fry in olive oil for few minutes. Serve warm. You can add some salt if you like.

Nutritional values per 100g:

Carbohydrates 0.9g

Sugar 0.45g

Protein 12g

Total fat 12.4g

Sodium 156mg

Potassium 117.5mg

Calcium 4.4mg

Iron 7.37mg

Vitamins (vitamin A; B-6; D; D2; D3)

Calories 156

27. Shrimps in tomato sauce

Ingredients:

2 cups of frozen shrimps

1 large tomato

1 tsp of dried basil

2 cloves of garlic

3 tbsp of olive oil

salt to taste

Preparation:

Grill frozen shrimps in a barbecue pan without oil. Wash and cut tomato into small pieces, add chopped basil, chopped garlic and olive oil. Cook it for 5-6 minutes (add some water if necessary). Pour the sauce over the grilled shrimps. Serve with lettuce.

Nutritional values per 100g:

Carbohydrates 7.9g

Sugar 4.2g

Protein 28g

Total fat (good monounsaturated fat) 1.32g

Sodium 131mg

Potassium 269.5mg

Calcium 8.7mg

Iron 4.37mg

Vitamins (vitamin A; B-6; B-12; C; D; D2; D3; K; Riboflavin; Niacin; Thiamin; K)

Calories 164

28. Lettuce salad

Ingredients:

1 bunch of lettuce

1 tbsp of olive oil

1 tsp of lemon juice

Preparation:

Wash and cut the lettuce, add olive oil and lemon juice. It is the best to prepare this salad before serving a meal. Don't let it stand long.

Nutritional values per 1 cup:

Carbohydrates 1.2g

Sugar 0.3g

Protein 1.7g

Total fat (good monounsaturated fat) 1.4g

Sodium 19mg

Potassium 132mg

Calcium 1.4mg

Iron 2.3mg

Vitamins (vitamin A; B-6; B-12; C;K)

Calories 25

29. Coriander salad

Ingredients:

1 cup of chopped coriander

1 boiled egg

2 cups of cherry tomatoes

1 tsp of tumeric

2 tbsp of olive oil

1 tsp of lemon sauce

salt to taste

Preparation:

Wash and cut cherry tomatoes and mix with coriander. Add tumeric, olive oil and lemon sauce.

Nutritional values for one cup:

Carbohydrates 14.2g

Sugar 8.9g

Protein 10g

Total fat (good monounsaturated fat) 9.6g

Sodium 122.2 mg

Potassium 81mg

Calcium 45.5mg

Iron 0.37mg

Vitamins (vitamin A; B-6; B-12; C; D; D2; D3; K; Riboflavin; Niacin; Thiamin; K)

Calories 55

30. Fried eggs with chopped mint

Ingredients:

3 eggs

1 tbsp of olive oil

1 tbsp of chopped mint

1 cup of cherry tomatoes

1 small onion

pepper to taste

salt to taste

Preparation:

Cut the vegetables into small pieces and fry in large saucepan on a low temperature for about 15 minutes. Wait for the water to evaporate. Beat the eggs and add chopped mint. Mix with vegetables, add olive oil and fry for few minutes. Before serving add some salt and pepper to taste.

Nutritional values per 100 g:

Carbohydrates 8.1g

Sugar 4g

Protein 28g

Total fat (good monounsaturated fat) 11.9g

Sodium 176mg

Potassium 174mg

Calcium 17.9mg

Iron 1.5mg

Vitamins (vitamin A; B-6; B-12; C; D; D2; D3; K; Riboflavin; Niacin; Thiamin; K)

Calories 194

31. Veal chop with chopped cloves

Ingredients:

2 large veal chops

1 cup of chopped cloves

4 tbsp of olive oil

1 tbsp of dried parsley

1 tsp of rosemary

1 tsp of red pepper

1 tbsp of lemon juice

Preparation:

Mix well the cloves, olive oil, parsley and rosemary to get a nice sauce. Wash the steak and put it in a small baking tray. Add sauce and bake for 15-20 minutes at 300 degrees. Remove from the oven, sprinkle with pepper and lemon juice. Decorate with few parsley leaves. Allow it to cool for about 10 minutes.

Nutritional values per 100g:

Carbohydrates 8.2g

Sugar 4.9g

Protein 22g

Total fat 9.6g

Sodium 97.2 mg

Potassium 381mg

Calcium 4.5mg

Iron 5.3mg

Vitamins (vitamin A; B-6; B-12; C; D; D2; D3; K; Riboflavin; Niacin; Thiamin; K)

Calories 216

32. Tomato soup

Ingredients:

1 cup of tomato sauce

2 egg whites

2 cups of water

2 cloves of garlic

2 tbsp of olive oil

1tsp of dried marjoram

chopped parsley

Preparation:

Fry finely chopped garlic in oil. Stir in tomato sauce mixed with water. Add parsley and let it boil. Serve with marjoram.

Nutritional values per 150ml:

Carbohydrates 6.8g

Sugar 3.9g

Protein 7g

Total fat (good monounsaturated fat) 0.6g

Sodium 190.2 mg

Potassium 112mg

Calcium 0.5mg

Iron 2.3mg

Vitamins (vitamin A; C)

Calories 30

33. Grilled zucchini with chopped basil and mint

Ingredients:

1 large zucchini

¼ cup of chopped basil

¼ cup of chopped mint

1 tbsp of olive oil

¼ glass of water,

pepper to taste

Preparation:

Cook spices in water and add pepper for 2-3 minutes. Peel and cut zucchini into three slices. Grill it in a barbecue pan with olive oil. Add mint and basil. Fry until all the water evaporates. You can add some lemon juice before serving, but this is optional.

Nutritional values for 1 slice:

Carbohydrates 3.8g

Sugar 2g

Protein 2.9 g

Total fat 0.9g

Sodium 2.76 mg

Potassium 343mg

Calcium 0.27mg

Iron 0.3mg

Vitamins (vitamin A; B-6; B-12; C; D:K)

Calories 23

34. Chopped veal soup with vegetables

Ingredients:

1 thick veal steak

2 large carrots

½ cup of chopped parsley

1 large tomato

¼ tsp of pepper

1 small onion

Preparation:

Wash the meat and put it in a pot. Pour water and cook until meat is tender. Meanwhile, clean and cut the vegetables into small cubes. When the meat is cooked, remove it from the pan and cut it into small cubes. Mix with vegetables, return to the water and cook until carrots are tender. Add seasoning and serve.

Nutritional values per 1 cup:

Carbohydrates 3g

Sugar 2.1g

Protein 22 g

Total fat 5.7g

Sodium 71 mg

Potassium 148mg

Calcium 2.2mg

Iron 4.3mg

Vitamins (vitamin A; B-6; B-12; C; D; D2; D3; K; Riboflavin; Niacin; Thiamin; K)

Calories 112

35. Lamb cutlet with hazelnut sauce

Ingredients:

1 medium lamb cutlet

½ cup of hazelnuts

1 tsp of curry

1 tbsp of olive oil

pepper to taste

Preparation:

Wash the cutlet and cook in water 15-20 minutes. Remove from pot and drain, but keep the water. Make a sauce with olive oil, curry, hazelnuts and pepper. Spread the sauce over cutlet, add some meat water and bake at 300 degrees for 15-20 minutes.

Nutritional values per 100g:

Carbohydrates 4.7g

Sugar 4.1g

Protein 29 g

Total fat 11.8g

Sodium 137 mg

Potassium 239mg

Calcium 2.9mg

Iron 2.16mg

Vitamins (vitamin A; B-6; B-12; C; D; D2; D3; K; Riboflavin; Niacin; Thiamin; K)

Calories 213

36. Grilled red pepper

Ingredients:

1 large red pepper

1 tbsp of olive oil

2 cloves of garlic

chopped parsley

Preparation:

Mix olive oil with garlic and parsley. Spread the sauce over paprika and bake in barbecue pan on low temperature for about 10-15 minutes.

Nutritional values per 100g:

Carbohydrates 6.2g

Sugar 4.4g

Protein 2g

Total fat 0.8g

Sodium 7 mg

Potassium 215mg

Calcium 2.8mg

Iron 2. 6mg

Vitamins (vitamin A; B-6; B-12; C; D;
Riboflavin; Niacin; Thiamin; K)

Calories 38

37. Eggplant pate

Ingredients:

1 large eggplant

6 egg whites

1 tsp of mustard

1 tsp of non-fat mayonnaise

2 cloves of garlic

1 tsp of parsley

¼ cup of water

1 tsp of olive oil

Preparation:

Note: The amount of eggplant and water can vary greatly depending on the type of eggplant and ways of preparing this pate. Eggplant baked in the oven will be dry, but it will be tastier and less bitter. Eggplant cleaned and "cooked" in a microwave will be lighter, with more fluid and a little more bitter, but ready in no time.

Peel the eggplant, cut into cubes and cook together in a covered, fireproof dish in the microwave for about 5 minutes. Or, bake in a conventional oven, peel the bark, well drain of water. Add water and blend eggplant with stick-blender.

Mix mayonnaise with egg whites and olive oil. Add eggplant and blend it together.

Add finely chopped garlic and mustard. This way you can get approximately one big jar of pate. It is excellent as a spread or as a side dish. Perfect with chicken and turkey.

Nutritional values per 100g:

Carbohydrates 12.9g

Sugar 6g

Protein 17g

Total fat 3.4g

Sodium 154mg

Potassium 132.5mg

Calcium 10.4mg

Iron 3.37mg

Vitamins (vitamin A; B-6; B-12; C; D; D2; D3; K; Riboflavin; Niacin; Thiamin; K)

Calories 71

38. Stewed beef and cabbage

Ingredients:

1 large beefsteak

1 cup of chopped cabbage, cooked

¼ tsp of pepper

2 tbsp of olive oil

½ cup of water

Preparation:

Cut meat into small pieces. Put in a pot and cook on a low temperature, in olive oil until tender. Add some water if necessary. When the meat tender, add cabbage and pepper. Stew on low temperature for at least 40 minutes.

Nutritional values per 100g:

Carbohydrates 8.1g

Sugar 3.2g

Protein 36.1 g

Total fat 6.9g

Sodium 157 mg

Potassium 499mg

Calcium 19.9mg

Iron 5.9mg

Vitamins (vitamin A; B-6; B-12; C; D; D2; D3; K;Thiamin; K)

Calories 234

39. Broccoli soup

Ingredients:

1 cup of broccoli

1 small carrot

1 small onion

little salt

pepper to taste

1 tbsp of coconut oil

Preparation:

Wash the onions and carrots, but do not chop them. Put them together with the broccoli in salted water and cook. When the vegetables are done, put them all together in a blender. Remaining vegetable water heat to boiling point and stir with a little oil. Cook until the mixture thickens, add the vegetables and cook for another 5-7 minutes. Serve warm.

Nutritional values for 1 cup:

Carbohydrates 15g

Sugar 5.2g

Protein 7.2 g

Total fat 4.1g

Sodium 887 mg

Potassium 376mg

Calcium 25.5mg

Iron 1.2mg

Vitamins (vitamin A;C)

Calories 120

40. Lettuce and tuna salad

Ingredients:

1 bunch of lettuce

3 cans of tuna without oil

1 tbsp of lemon juice

2 large onions

2 large tomatoes

5 olives

Preparation:

Wash and cut lettuce. Mix it with tuna. Peel and cut the onion, cut the tomato, mix with tuna and lettuce. Add lemon juice and olives.

Nutritional values for 1 cup:

Carbohydrates 19.4g

Sugar 12g

Protein 31.2g

Total fat (good monounsaturated fat) 11.5g

Sodium 141mg

Potassium 86.1mg

Calcium 43.2mg

Iron 0.31mg

Vitamins (vitamin A; B-6; B-12; C; D; D2; D3; K; Riboflavin; Niacin; Thiamin; K)

Calories 71

41. Grilled trout fillets with parsley

Ingredients:

3 thick trout fillets

1 tbsp of parsley

3 tbsp of olive oil

6 cloves of garlic

Preparation:

Mix chopped garlic with parsley and olive oil. Spread it over fish and fry in a barbecue pan for about 15-20 minutes, on both sides. Remove from the pan and use a kitchen paper to soak the excess oil.

Nutritional values per 100g:

Carbohydrates 0.2g

Sugar 0

Protein 25.2 g

Total fat 6.6g

Sodium 113.8 mg

Potassium 61mg

Calcium 29mg

Iron 0.33mg

Vitamins (vitamin A; B-6; B-12; C; D; D2; D3; K; Riboflavin; Niacin; Thiamin; K)

Calories 170

42. Cauliflower soup

Ingredients:

1 cup of cauliflower

1 small carrot

1 small onion

little pepper

1 tbsp of oil

Preparation:

Wash the onions and carrots, but do not chop them. Put them together with the cauliflower in water and cook. When the vegetables are done, put them all together in a blender. Remaining vegetable water heat to boiling point and stir with a little oil. Cook until the mixture thickens, add the vegetables and cook for another 5-7 minutes. Serve warm.

Nutritional values for 1 cup:

Carbohydrates 13g

Sugar 4.2g

Protein 6.2 g

Total fat 4.4g

Sodium 862 mg

Potassium 366mg

Calcium 24.1mg

Iron 2mg

Vitamins (vitamin A;C)

Calories 118

43. Tomato omelet

Ingredients:

3 eggs

1 large tomato

1 small onion

1 tsp of olive oil

salt to taste

Preparation:

Wash and cut tomato. Peel and cut the onion. Fry tomato and onion in olive oil for about 10-15 minutes, on a low temperature. Remove from the heat when the water evaporates. Add eggs and mix well. Fry for another 2 minutes.

Nutritional values per 100 g:

Carbohydrates 6.1g

Sugar 2g

Protein 20g

Total fat (good monounsaturated fat) 12g

Sodium 176mg

Potassium 173mg

Calcium 15.9mg

Iron 1.9mg

Vitamins (vitamin A; B-6; B-12; C)

Calories 184

44. Grilled salmon fillet

Ingredients:

1 large salmon fillet

1 tbsp of lemon juice

2 tbsp of olive oil

1 tbsp of ground chili pepper

Preparation:

Wash the fillet and pat dry using a kitchen paper. Sprinkle some lemon juice on it and fry in a small barbecue pan for about 15-20 minutes, on a very high temperature. Remove from the pan and soak the excess oil with a kitchen paper. Add ground chili pepper before serving.

Nutritional values per 100 g:

Carbohydrates 2.9

Sugar 0.8g

Protein 24g

Total fat (good monounsaturated fat) 14.6g

Sodium 63mg

Potassium 374mg

Calcium 0.9mg

Iron 1.8mg

Vitamins (vitamin A; B-6; B-12; C)

Calories 220

45. Mixed vegetable salad:

Ingredients:

1 bunch of lettuce

1 small carrot

1 medium tomato

1 medium onion

1 small cucumber

1 medium eggplant

1 medium zucchini

1 tbsp of olive oil

1 tsp of lemon juice

Preparation:

Peel and cut eggplant and zucchini. Fry it in olive oil for 8-10 minutes. Remove from pan and soak excess oil with kitchen paper. Meanwhile, wash and cut vegetables into small pieces. Mix eggplant and zucchini with other vegetables and season with olive oil and lemon juice.

Nutritional values for one cup:

Carbohydrates 12.3g

Sugar 8.9g

Protein 11.2 g

Total fat (good monounsaturated fat) 6.5g

Sodium 176.3 mg

Potassium 95mg

Calcium 63.5mg

Iron 0.74mg

Vitamins (vitamin A; B-6; B-12; C; D; D2; D3; K; Riboflavin; Niacin; Thiamin; K)

Calories 51

46. Grilled calamari in curry sauce

Ingredients:

1 cup of frozen calamari rings

¼ cup of water

1 tsp of curry

2 tbsp of olive oil

2 cloves of garlic

1 tsp of chopped parsley

Preparation:

Make a sauce with chopped water, garlic, parsley, curry and olive oil. Fry calamari rings in a barbecue pan without oil for 7-10 minutes, on a medium temperature. You want to get a nice golden color. Add the sauce to barbecue pan with calamari and fry for few more minutes. You can add some more water if your sauce is too thick.

Nutritional values per 100g:

Carbohydrates 0.2g

Sugar 0g

Protein 19.8 g

Total fat (good monounsaturated fat) 2.8g

Sodium 96.3 mg

Potassium 0.3mg

Calcium 1.5mg

Iron 0.7mg

Vitamins (vitamin A; BD; D2; K)

Calories 92

47. Grilled sardines

Ingredients:

1 small pack (200g) of frozen sardines

4 cloves of garlic

4 tbsp of olive oil

3 tsp of tumeric

½ tsp of salt

Preparation:

Defrost and wash sardines. Make a garlic sauce with garlic, olive oil and tumeric. Spread it over sardines and fry in a barbecue pan without extra oil for about 20 minutes on a medium temperature. They should have golden-brow color before serving. Salt to taste.

Nutritional values per 100g:

Carbohydrates 0.2g

Sugar 0g

Protein 19 g

Total fat (good monounsaturated fat) 6g

Sodium 225.3 mg

Potassium 3mg

Calcium 3.5mg

Iron 3.2mg

Vitamins (vitamin A; B-6; D; D2; D3; K; Riboflavin; Niacin; Thiamin; K)

Calories 130

48. Banana shake

Ingredients:

1 large banana

2 egg whites

1.5 cup of water

1 tsp of vanilla extract

1 tbsp of agave syrup

Preparation:

Peel and chop banana into small cubes. Combine with other ingredients in a blender and mix for 30 seconds, until smooth mixture. Keep in the refrigerator and serve cold.

Nutritional values for 1 glass:

Carbohydrates 8g

Sugar 4.9g

Protein 10.2g

Total fat 2.67g

Sodium 74mg

Potassium 512.9mg

Calcium 79mg

Iron 1.88mg

Vitamins (Vitamin B-6; B-12; D; D-D2+D3)

Calories 56

49. Grilled green peppers

Ingredients:

2 green peppers

1 tbsp of olive oil

2 cloves of garlic

chopped parsley

Preparation:

Mix the olive oil with garlic and parsley. Spread the sauce over peppers and fry in a barbecue pan on a low temperature for about 10-15 minutes. Stir constantly.

Nutritional values per 100g:

Carbohydrates 5g

Sugar 2.2g

Protein 1.8 g

Total fat 0.4g

Sodium 4.3 mg

Potassium 191mg

Calcium 2.5mg

Iron 1.8mg

Vitamins (vitamin A; B-6; B-12; C; D; D2; D3; K; Riboflavin; Niacin; Thiamin; K)

Calories 27

50. Seafood salad

Ingredients:

1 small pack (200g) of frozen mixed seafood

3 tbsp of olive oil

1 medium onion

¼ tsp of salt

¼ cup of water (optional)

Preparation

Fry frozen seafood without oil until tender (try the octopus, it takes the most time to tender). You can add some water if necessary. Remove from frying pan and allow it to cool for about an hour. Peel and finely chop the onion. Mix it with seafood and add olive oil. This salad is best cold. Let it stand in the refrigerator for few hours before serving.

Nutritional values per 1 cup:

Carbohydrates 3.45g

Sugar 1.68g

Protein 25.8 g

Total fat 16.4g

Sodium 827mg

Potassium 453mg

Calcium 13.5mg

Iron 10mg

Vitamins (Vitamin C; B-6; B-12; A-RAE; A-IU; E; D; D-D2+D3; K; Thianin; Riboflavin; Niacin)

Calories 280

51. Grilled zucchini with garlic

Ingredients:

1 large zucchini

4 cloves of garlic

1 tbsp of olive oil

¼ tsp of salt

Preparation:

Peel and cut zucchini into thick slices. Chop garlic and fry it for few minutes in olive oil, until nice gold color. Add zucchini and fry for another 10 minutes on a low temperature. Sprinkle with some chopped parsley before serving. Salt to taste.

Nutritional values for 1 slice:

Carbohydrates 3.6g

Sugar 1.9g

Protein 2.9 g

Total fat 0.9g

Sodium 2.21 mg

Potassium 354mg

Calcium 0.12mg

Iron 0.2mg

Vitamins (vitamin A; B-6; B-12; C; D:K)

Calories 25

52. Baked apples

Ingredients:

2 large apples

1 tsp of cinnamon

Preparation:

Bake the apples at 300 degrees for 15 minutes. Sprinkle with cinnamon before serving.

Nutritional values per 100g:

Carbohydrates 14.8g

Sugar 10g

Protein 0.4 g

Total fat 0.3g

Sodium 1.7mg

Potassium 108mg

Calcium 0mg

Iron 0mg

Vitamins (vitamin A; C)

Calories 53

53. Grilled steak with pineapple slices

Ingredients:

1 large steak

7 pineapple slices

1 tsp of ginger

little water

pepper to taste

Preparation:

Fry pineapple slices for 5-10 minutes, slightly adding a little water. Remove pineapple slices from a frying pan and fry the steak in the same frying pan for 15-20 minutes. You can add some water while frying steak. Serve with pineapple slices and sprinkle with ginger. Pepper to taste

Nutritional values per 100g:

Carbohydrates 3.8g

Sugar 2.1g

Protein 32.9 g

Total fat 4.9g

Sodium 64 mg

Potassium 413mg

Calcium 0mg

Iron 17.8mg

Vitamins (vitamin A; B-6; B-12; C; D)

Calories 182

54. Cooked cauliflower in mint sauce

Ingredients:

1 medium cauliflower

1 tbsp of chopped mint leaves

1 tsp of ginger

1 tbsp of agave syrup

Preparation:

Clean and cut cauliflower into medium cubes. Cook it in water until tender. Remove from pot and drain well. Meanwhile, make a sauce with agave syrup, ginger and mint, by combining all the ingredients in a small bowl. Pour it over cauliflower and allow it to cool for a while before serving.

Nutritional values per 100g:

Carbohydrates 6.8g

Sugar 2.8g

Protein 1.9 g

Total fat 0.4g

Sodium 31 mg

Potassium 301mg

Calcium 2.7mg

Iron 2.3mg

Vitamins (vitamin C; K)

Calories 29

55. Mushroom soup

Ingredients:

1 cup of fresh button mushrooms

1 small carrot

1 small onion

¼ tsp of pepper

1 tbsp of oil

Preparation:

Wash the onions and carrots, but do not chop them. Put them together in a large pot, add water to cover the vegetables and cook until tender. When the vegetables are done, mix them with mushrooms and put all together in a blender. Remaining vegetable water heat to boiling point and stir with a little oil. Cook until the mixture thickens, add the vegetables and cook for another 5-7 minutes. You can decorate it with little parsley.

Nutritional values for 1 cup:

Carbohydrates 3.3g

Sugar 0.2g

Protein 1.9 g

Total fat 2.6g

Sodium 340 mg

Potassium 31mg

Calcium 0mg

Iron 0mg

Vitamins (vitamin D;K)

Calories 41

56. Trout fillet with almond and tumeric sauce

Ingredients:

1 thin slice of trout fillet

1 tsp of tumeric

1 tbsp of olive oil

½ cup of almonds

1 tsp of dried rosemary

¼ tsp of pepper

Preparation:

Wash and dry the fillet. Sprinkle with tumeric and fry in hot oil for few minutes on each side. Remove from frying pan. Make a sauce with almonds, olive oil, rosemary and pepper. Pour the sauce over the fillet and fry for another few minutes, until golden brown color.

Nutritional values per 100g:

Carbohydrates 3.7g

Sugar 0.2g

Protein 25g

Total fat 8.6g

Sodium 62 mg

Potassium 263mg

Calcium 10mg

Iron 2.5mg

Vitamins (vitamin A; B-6; B-12; C; D:K)

Calories 173

57. Trout soup

Ingredients:

1 large trout

2 small carrots

1 tbsp of olive oil

1 tsp of dried parsley

dill to taste

Preparation:

Wash and clean the fish (remove all bones). Cook the fish in a large pot for about 20. After the fish is done, add a little olive oil (just to cover the bottom). Fry chopped carrots for few minutes and add water, parsley and dill. Cook for another 15 minutes. After about 15 minutes add the fish (whole or cut into large chunks). Put in each plate 1 tsp of olive oil and pour the soup.

Nutritional values per 1 cup:

Carbohydrates 3.4g

Sugar 0.9g

Protein 5.9 g

Total fat 2g

Sodium 365 mg

Potassium 123mg

Calcium 2.3mg

Iron 2.3mg

Vitamins (vitamin A; B-6; B-12; C)

Calories 46

58. Cucumber salad

Ingredients:

3 large cucumbers

6 tbsp of grated walnuts

3 tbsp of sesame seeds oil

Preparation:

Peel and cut the cucumbers into thin slices. Season with sesame seed oil and sprinkle with grated walnuts.

Nutritional values per 100g:

Carbohydrates 6.8g

Sugar 2.7g

Protein 5.9 g

Total fat 4.9g

Sodium 5.76 mg

Potassium 213mg

Calcium 5.27mg

Iron 2.1mg

Vitamins (vitamin A; B-6; B-12; C; D:K)

Calories 34

59. Grilled mushrooms with garlic sauce

Ingredients:

3 cups of fresh button mushrooms

6 cloves of garlic

3 tbsp of olive oil

¼ tsp of pepper

Preparation:

Fry mushrooms without oil in a barbecue pan on a low temperature until all the water evaporates. Meanwhile, chop garlic, add to frying pan and mix with mushrooms. Fry for few more minutes. Sprinkle with olive oil before serving. Add some pepper to taste. Serve warm.

Nutritional values for one cup:

Carbohydrates 5.2g

Sugar 1.3g

Protein 8.2 g

Total fat (good monounsaturated fat) 2.3g

Sodium 47.3 mg

Potassium 25.1mg

Calcium 13.1mg

Iron 0.61mg

Vitamins (vitamin A; B-6; B-12; C; D; D2; D3;
K; Riboflavin; Niacin; Thiamin; K)

Calories 98

60. Apple and carrot balls with cinnamon

Ingredients:

5 large apples

3 large carrots

6 tsp of cinnamon

6 tsp of agave syrup

3 tsp of lemon juice

Preparation:

Peel and grate apples and carrots. Combine with other ingredients in a blender to get a smooth mixture. Make little balls and allow them to cool them in the refrigerator for few hours.

You can add grated walnuts or almonds to this recipe. That is optional, but it will increase the proteins.

Nutritional values per 100g:

Carbohydrates 17.2g

Sugar 15.3g

Protein 9.1 g

Total fat (good monounsaturated fat) 2.3g

Sodium 147.4 mg

Potassium 625mg

Calcium 13.1mg

Iron 11.61mg

Vitamins (vitamin A; B-6; B-12; C; D; D2; D3; K; Riboflavin; Niacin; Thiamin; K)

Calories 78

61. Grilled eggplant with parsley

Ingredients:

1 small eggplant

½ cup of chopped parsley

1 tsp of olive oil

Preparation:

Peel the eggplant and cut into slices. Bake it in a barbecue pan without oil. When done, spread olive oil over it, sprinkle with parsley.

Nutritional values per slice:

Carbohydrates 7.9g

Sugar .4

Protein 7.2g

Total fat 2.21g

Sodium 53mg

Potassium 29.1mg

Calcium 13.1mg

Iron 0.38mg

Vitamins (vitamin A; B-6; B-12; C; D; D2; D3; K; Riboflavin; Niacin; Thiamin; K)

Calories 52

62. Steak salad with mushrooms

Ingredients:

1 large steak

3 cups of button mushrooms

6 tbsp of chopped parsley

1 bunch of lettuce

1 large tomato

1 large onion

1 large cucumber

4 tbsp of olive oil

Preparation:

Fry the steak without oil for 15-20 minutes. Remove from pan and cut it into medium sized pieces. Fry the mushrooms, but don't cut them. Wash and peel vegetables, mix with steak and mushrooms. Season with little olive or sesame oil.

Nutritional values for one cup:

Carbohydrates 18.6g

Sugar 11.3g

Protein 21.9g

Total fat (good monounsaturated fat)
14.2g

Sodium 153.3 mg

Potassium 89.8mg

Calcium 49.9mg

Iron 0.42mg

Vitamins (vitamin A; B-6; B-12; C; D; D2;
D3; K; Riboflavin; Niacin; Thiamin; K)

Calories 79

63. Fruit shake

Ingredients:

1 cup of strawberries

1 large banana

1 slice of watermelon

½ tsp of cinnamon

½ cup of water

¼ cup of ground walnuts

Preparation:

Mix ingredients in a blender for about 30 seconds. Sprinkle with cinnamon and allow it to cool in the refrigerator for about 30 minutes. Serve with ice.

Nutritional values for 1 glass:

Carbohydrates 10.67g

Sugar 8.11g

Protein 8.65g

Total fat 2.54g

Sodium 95mg

Potassium 159.6mg

Calcium 93mg

Iron 1.03mg

Vitamins (Vitamin C total ascorbic acid; B-6; B-12; A-RAE; A-IU; E-alpha-tocopherol; D; K-phylloquinone; Thianin; Riboflavin; Niacin)

Calories 74.6

64. Veal cutlet with almonds

Ingredients:

1 veal cutlet

½ cup of grated almonds

¼ tsp of pepper

1 tsp of sesame oil

½ cup of water

Preparation:

Mix almonds, pepper and water. Cook it for about 10 minutes. Remove from heat and cool it. Wash and dry cutlet. Fry it in oil for about 15-20 minutes. Add almond sauce before serving.

Nutritional values per 100g:

Carbohydrates 4.6g

Sugar 4.2g

Protein 29.6 g

Total fat 11.4g

Sodium 133 mg

Potassium 234mg

Calcium 2.3mg

Iron 2.13mg

Vitamins (vitamin A; B-6; B-12; C; D; D2; D3; K; Riboflavin; Niacin; Thiamin; K)

Calories 217

65. Spinach omelet

Ingredients:

1 cup of chopped spinach

2 eggs

olive oil for frying

Preparation:

Cook spinach in salted water until tender. Remove from pan and drain. Fry in olive oil for 5-6 minutes and add eggs. Mix well and serve warm.

Nutritional values per 100g:

Carbohydrates 0.98g

Sugar 0.44g

Protein 12.1g

Total fat 14.4g

Sodium 256mg

Potassium 217.4mg

Calcium 5.6mg

Iron 11.37mg

Vitamins (vitamin A; B-6; D; D2; D3)

Calories 143

66. Squids stuffed with walnuts

Ingredients:

2 large squids

½ cup of grated walnuts

1 tsp of lemon juice

½ tsp of ginger

1 tbsp of olive oil

Preparation:

Wash and clean the squids. Mix walnuts, lemon juice and ginger and stuff squids. Place in greased pan and cover with baking foil. Bake for 20 minutes in preheated oven, at 200 degrees. Remove the foil and bake for another 5-10 minutes.

Nutritional values per 100g:

Carbohydrates 0.2g

Sugar 0g

Protein 19.8 g

Total fat (good monounsaturated fat) 2.8g

Sodium 96.3 mg

Potassium 0.3mg

Calcium 1.5mg

Iron 0.7mg

Vitamins (vitamin A; BD; D2; K)

Calories 92

67. Tomato and garlic soup

Ingredients:

1 cup of tomato sauce

2 cups of water

2 cloves of garlic

2 tbsp of olive oil

1 tsp of dried marjoram

Preparation:

Fry finely chopped garlic in oil for about 10 minutes. Stir in tomato sauce mixed with water. Let it boil for 7-10 minutes. Serve with marjoram.

Nutritional values per 150ml:

Carbohydrates 7.9g

Sugar 4.1g

Protein 7.9g

Total fat 0.9g

Sodium 195.3 mg

Potassium 117mg

Calcium 0.3mg

Iron 2.8mg

Vitamins (vitamin A; C)

Calories 39

68. Lamb cutlet with basil

Ingredients:

1 thick lamb cutlet

1 tsp of chopped basil

pepper to taste

1 tbsp of sesame oil

Preparation:

Fry cutlet in sesame oil for 15 minutes. Remove from pan and soak up excess oil. Sprinkle with pepper and basil.

Nutritional values per 100g:

Carbohydrates 5.9g

Sugar 4.5g

Protein 29.3 g

Total fat 11.9g

Sodium 129 mg

Potassium 241mg

Calcium 2.93mg

Iron 2.17mg

Vitamins (vitamin A; B-6; B-12; C; D; D2; D3; K; Riboflavin; Niacin; Thiamin; K)

Calories 210

69. Grilled mushrooms in tomato sauce

Ingredients:

1 cup of button mushrooms

1 large tomato

1 tsp of olive oil

2 cloves of garlic

1 tbsp of fresh basil

Preparation:

Wash and cut tomato. Chop garlic and mix with tomato and fresh basil. Cook it in olive oil and little water for about 10-15 minutes, on low temperature. Grill mushrooms without oil in a barbecue pan for 5 minutes. Add to tomato sauce and mix well.

Nutritional values for one cup:

Carbohydrates 5.1g

Sugar 2.7g

Protein 6.1 g

Total fat 1.8g

Sodium 46.1 mg

Potassium 24.1mg

Calcium 13.5mg

Iron 0.62mg

Vitamins (vitamin A; B-6; B-12; C; D; D2; D3; K; Riboflavin; Niacin; Thiamin; K)

Calories 108

70. Shrimp skewers

Ingredients:

6 frozen shrimps

6 cherry tomatoes

6 eggplant cubes

6 green pepper cubes

olive oil

½ tsp of oregano

2 wooden sticks

Preparation:

Put the ingredients on 2 wooden sticks – 1 shrimp, 1 tomato, 1 eggplant cube, 1 green pepper cube. Repeat the process until you use all the ingredients. Sprinkle with olive oil and oregano and fry in a barbecue pan for 5-10 minutes.

Nutritional values per 100g:

Carbohydrates 7.1g

Sugar 4.3g

Protein 29g

Total fat (good monounsaturated fat) 1.42g

Sodium 132mg

Potassium 279.1mg

Calcium 8.4mg

Iron 4.32mg

Vitamins (vitamin A; B-6; B-12; C; D; D2; D3; K; Riboflavin; Niacin; Thiamin; K)

Calories 154

Chapter 7:

Meditating For Maximum

Mental Toughness in Marathons

Meditating to reach your maximum potential will depend on your ability to focus on a thought or problem and stay focused for as long as necessary to solve the problem or until you realize your objective. This will create confidence and self-conviction for future tasks you may need to accomplish.

When you meditate and want to achieve maximum results you will need to follow these exact steps every time. If you change or eliminate any step, you will end up changing the outcome of the meditation session.

These steps are:

1st: Find a quiet place where you won't be disturbed.

2nd: Place a mat, towel, blanket, or chair where you are planning to meditate.

3rd: Make sure you had a light meal or snack about an hour before meditating.

4th: Choose a position in which you will be comfortable in for the entire session. This could be: sitting on a chair, lying down on a mat, sitting in a Burmese, Lotus or butterfly position, kneeling on a mat, or any other comfortable meditation position mentioned before.

5th: Begin your breathing pattern. If you want to calm and relax yourself you should choose to breathe more air out than you do air in (except if you are doing mindfulness meditation as you should not try to control your breathing but instead simply feel the air going into your lungs and then out into your surroundings.). For example, breathe in 4 seconds and then breathe out for 6 seconds. When trying to energize yourself because you feel too relaxed or just woke up, you would breathe more air in than out in a specific ratio which you can decide beforehand. For example, breathe 5 seconds in and 3 seconds out. Remember each sequence of breathing needs to be repeated at least 4 to 6 times to allow your breathing to slow the mind down and get you in a state of calmness to best meditate. For all breathing patterns you will breathe in through your nose and out through your mouth, except for mindfulness meditation which will be in and out through your nose only as the focus is not on your breathing.

6th: Once you are done completing your breathing patterns in the manner explained in the breathing patterns chapter, you should begin to focus on something you want to obtain, achieve, or simply preview in your mind. Focus on this for as long as possible. Short sessions give you shorter lasting results while longer sessions tend to help you maintain this level of concentration even after you're done meditating. All marathon runners know that when it's time to perform, (especially when under pressure), they need to stay focused and being able to do this for a longer period of time without losing concentration will permit them to outperform the competition. **This is the difference between champions and the rest!**

7th: This thought should now evolve to a short or long mental movie clip you are creating in your mind to help you achieve what you want in your mind first, with the goal to eventually make it happen in a real life situation. Be as specific as possible and stay relaxed in the process. This seventh step adds visualizing to the process but there's nothing wrong with that as it can only benefit you but it's necessary if you just want to keep it simple.

8th: Marathon runners need to use breathing to finish their meditation sessions to end as they began. If you don't have to compete on the same day, you can use slow breathing patterns such as the example below:

Normal slow breathing pattern: Start by taking air in through your nose slowly and counting to 5. Then, release slowly counting back down from 5 to 1. You should repeat this process 4 to 10 times until you feel completely relaxed and ready to meditate. Marathon runners should focus on breathing in through the nose and out through the mouth for this type of breathing pattern.

If you have to compete the same day you should energize your mind and body at the end by using fast breathing patterns such as the one below:

Normal fast breathing pattern: Start by taking air in through your nose slowly and counting to 5. Then, release slowly counting back down from 3 to 1. You should repeat this process 6 to 10 times until you feel completely relaxed but energized. Marathon runners should focus on breathing in through the nose and out through the mouth for this type of breathing pattern.

For marathon runners who are doing mindfulness meditation, their sessions should end once they are done meditating as the focus behind this form of meditation is not breathing but instead to calm the mind and focus on a specific thought.

Chapter 8:

Mental Toughness through Meditating for Emotional Strength

The emotional strain behind every competition is overwhelming, tiring, and exhausting. Preparing yourself to overcome emotional stress is very important and necessary to overcome mental hurdles.

Some marathon runners are great when training but fall apart under emotional stress when competing, but meditating can improve your approach to this kind of stress.

Some will yell, scream, complain, lower their heads, show low self-esteem, appear with low energy, cry, or even be nervous. This is normal under pressure situations but it can be a problem easily fixed through meditation.

Let's look at some problems and solutions that you can focus on when meditating.

Why do I feel insecure when I am competing?

Insecurity can happen for a number of reasons. For some, its lack of preparation where you might feel you're not prepared to compete. For this problem simply prepare as much as you need to until you feel ready. Don't get pressured into competing if you're not ready.

For others, insecurity might come from comparing yourself too much with others instead of focusing on your results and improving off past results. Focus on seeing yourself improve through training and better preparation when you meditate.

Why do I get angry with myself and others when I am competing?

Anger is a common reaction for many marathon runners when they are under pressure and don't know what to do. Other times anger can be a result of frustration. Some people get angry with themselves, others with the competition, many with people close to them, and lastly at external conditions they have no control over.

When meditating, you can overcome this problem by trying to focus on accepting that there are things you have no control over and can only anticipate them and have an alternate plan if they occur. Accept weather conditions, noise, or delays which are possible situations which can happen but can have different consequences on you depending on your level of preparation.

There will also be circumstances in which you will have control over situations and can prevent getting angry.

If there is someone you prefer not having around when you compete, simply ask them politely to wait for you to finish and then can share the triumph with you later. They should understand if they truly desire the best for you and that's the way it should be.

When you feel angry because you're not competing the way you believe you could, meditation would definitely help you to plan things better by using your meditating time to prepare a path or a step by step process to follow that will give you the best possible chance to perform at your true potential.

Why am I so afraid during a competition?

Fear is one of the most common conditions all marathon runners suffer from. It's a human emotion in reaction to a threat. Fear comes in different forms and sizes. Some types of fear are based on events or things that don't really exist but are created in your mind. These are often things that could happen but might never happen at all. Let me repeat the last part "could happen but might never happen at all".

Fear of future outcomes are a waste of energy and will drain you emotionally. Future outcomes are a result of present planning and proper preparation. If you focus on results based goals and achieve them during competition, most of the time you will obtain your results based goals.

For example, focusing on being positive and adaptive no matter what the situation, will help you overcome difficult conditions and many times have a positive result at the end mainly because you did not stop believing in yourself and didn't give up.

Fear can also be due to a current threat that is small in nature but because you think so much on it you end up building it up to a huge problem and a huge fear. Never let this happen because you will make it impossible for your mind to overcome a situation like this. If your climbing a hill, don't look at it like Mount Everest because you'll want to quit before you even start.

Give each circumstance and problem the attention it deserves and no more. Meditate on focusing on one thing and once you are done with it focus on something else. You don't have to over analyze hundreds of outcomes when there might be a less than a 1% chance they might even happen.

When you meditate you try to see yourself in a different image. Use your mind to see yourself as you wish. For example, you could choose to see yourself as a confident, fearless, and aggressive person.

Don't give others more credit than their due and don't cut yourself short. Being overconfident is better than being fearful and being sure of yourself is better than being overconfident. Find the right balance and build that image in your mind then try to live that image on a daily basis.

I feel so nervous when I'm under pressure, why is this?

Being nervous can actually be a good thing as it can have a positive affect over your mind and body. How can nerves be good you ask? For some people, being nervous can bring out the best in themselves and compete better than they usually would. In other circumstances, your body might trigger adrenaline to naturally enhance your senses and physical capabilities.

Being nervous might also cause the opposite affect and make you freeze when you need to react. This is a huge and very obvious problem.

When meditating you often improve your breathing pattern skills and learn to control the flow of air in your body. This is a very useful skill that has a powerful effect on nervousness and your emotions in general.

Three things you can do when you're under pressure are:

1. Take deep breaths and slow your heart rate down. (Meditation will greatly improve this practice and better prepare you for when you're nervous).

2. Staying active (the opposite reaction would be to stay still or to "freeze" which is bad. Stay active doing whatever you need to be doing to help keep your cool. Some people chew gum or sun flower seeds, others move their feet, and some listen to music, while others try to distract themselves before competing by reading books or talking to others. There are many more ways of staying active but you have to choose one that's right for you.)

3. Thinking positive thoughts (Meditation is often used to slow the mind and relax the body which then allows your brain to concentrate on productive thoughts which should be positive. Use meditation to help you become more positive by practicing positive thinking in your sessions.)

Chapter 9:

Mental Toughness through Meditating For Improved Mental Strength

Being mentally tough can mean many things but for a marathon runner it means not falling under pressure and meeting any challenge head on with the power of the mind. As you become more and more advanced you will notice that your body can only take you so far and the mind is the one that has to take control over the future of your results. Being mentally tough will permit you to take control of these future results and push you to your limit thanks to the efforts made when meditating for mental toughness.

What does it mean to use meditation for mental toughness in marathons?

In marathons, mental toughness is a skill that needs to be developed over time but that will be reliable when it's time to perform. Mental toughness can be used in many ways.

Meditation can become the fastest path to mental toughness due to the non-physical skills you will develop and improve. It can be used to stay calm under pressure. It can also be used to enhance your performance. Lastly, it can be used to outlast the competition when you feel your body is can go no further.

Three examples of mental toughness skills that you could develop for marathons when meditating for mental toughness would be:

Using proper mental vocabulary

Most of us have inner conversations with ourselves and the words we use have a huge impact on our actions. Telling your body "not to give up" is an example of having a negative mental vocabulary. If you tell your body to "keep going", you would be using a positive mental vocabulary. With the first, your brain searches for key words and in this case it hears the words "give up" even though you are trying to force it to hear "not to give up". This is simply how the brain works. In the second example, the brain hears the key words "keep going" and continues going. Shorter isn't the solution, simply the key words you use. Stay away from using any words that could allow the brain to associate actions you don't want happening.

Projecting a confident image of yourself

By forcing yourself to stand straight, your hands to relax, your face to look more relaxed and self-assured, and showing the competition you are ready for whatever is up ahead, you will change how the mind approaches any conflicting situation and your potential results. This is true 10 out of every 10 times. Project a confident image of yourself and your brain will gear up for confident thoughts which will create confident actions.

Previewing your actions (Visualizing)

Doing things on pure instinct instead of having an idea of what would be the perfect way of doing them, are two completely different approaches to a circumstance but one can sometimes go right while the other will work out better much more often. Previewing your actions before doing them is similar to using visualizations but the difference is you will create the short mental image of what you want to do right before you do it.

INSTANT IMAGE, INSTANT ACTION. Close your eyes for 1, 2, or 3 seconds, if time allows add a few more seconds and see yourself perform the action you are trying to accomplish and then open your eyes and perform this action in that instant. You will notice you are much more precise with your actions than ever before.

Remember, when meditating for mental toughness, you are going to practice the skills detailed above so that you can apply them under mentally tough conditions and overcome those challenges that others struggle with.

Chapter 10:

Mental Toughness through Meditating For Problem Solving

What does it mean to meditate for problem solving?

Well, if you have a problem, your brain could have the solution but when you're busy thinking about a million things and doing another 10 at the same time consciously or unconsciously, this will be impossible.

By slowing down your thinking and calming your emotions through meditation and proper breathing techniques, it will be easier to focus on one problem at a time and find alternatives or possible solutions to fix the problem.

That's what meditation does best. It breaks things down to a simple idea or thought and concentrates only on this. These thoughts can be simply positive thoughts or ideas or they could be problems you need to find solutions for.

When you create a specific time to meditate, you are also creating time to solve a problem you are having which otherwise might not have a time dedicated to just it.

That's another positive result of meditating that most marathon runners never consider, and miss out on having any possibilities of finding alternatives to lifelong mistakes that are never corrected since they chose not to meditate.

What types of problems can I solve when meditating?

Any problem you might be having can be analyzed through the mind and sometimes you will find a solution immediately while other times it might take a lot longer or never at all. The brain has the capacity to find what you're looking for if you take the time to focus on it.

The real problem occurs when you don't take the time to dedicate yourself to finding a solution and giving it the proper attention it deserves.

Why is meditating for problem solving important to me?

As a marathon runner, you are constantly being challenged and pushed which in turn means you are constantly being given new problems to solve every second, minute, or moment. By not preparing yourself to overcome these new challenges, you are allowing luck to become more valuable than your mental capacity to solve problems. This should never be the case. Remember, "Luck comes to those who are prepared". Be prepared to get lucky instead.

Five things to take into account when problem solving are:

1. Never overanalyze a problem to the point where it becomes a bigger problem than it really is.
2. Always allow the mind to try again when you don't find a solution instantly when meditating. You might find a solution on the second or third time you meditate on the same problem.
3. Every problem has a solution. Meditating will help you search for a solution to a

problem but keep in mind that you might need someone else's input to better solve it so always be humble enough to accept advise or to seek out help.

4. Not all problems need to be solved. If something is so minute in size that it does not deserve any attention, than skip it and move on to the important stuff that will cause the biggest impact in your results.

5. Meditating will help you solve many problems but sometimes visualizing will take you a step further, which is often necessary when you need to see mental images and mental videos of what's really going on.

Remember, meditating for problem solving is a great use for meditation but not the only use. Use your time wisely when meditating so that you make the most of it since the mind will give you the best quality concentration for a specific time interval and then the rest of the time will not be as productive and that's when you know you're done and need to end the session.

Made in the USA
Monee, IL
05 November 2022

17186832R00125